W9-BGH-123

VALENTINE

Vol. 46, No. 1   February 1989

Publisher, Patricia A. Pingry
Executive Editor, Peggy Schaefer
Art Director, Patrick McRae
Production Manager, Jeff Wyatt
Editorial Assistant, Kathleen Gilbert
Copy Editors, Marian Hollyday
                      Rhonda Colburn

ISBN 0-8249-1069-9

IDEALS—Vol. 46, No.1 February 1989 IDEALS (ISSN 0019-137X) is published eight times a year: February, March, April, June, August, September, November, December by IDEALS PUBLISHING CORPORATION, Nelson Place at Elm Hill Pike, Nashville, Tenn. 37214. Second class postage paid at Nashville, Tennessee, and additional mailing offices. Copyright © 1989 by IDEALS PUBLISHING CORPORA-TION. POSTMASTER: Send address changes to Ideals, Post Office Box 148000, Nashville, Tenn. 37214-8000. All rights reserved. Title IDEALS registered U.S. Patent Office.

SINGLE ISSUE—$3.95
ONE-YEAR SUBSCRIPTION—eight consecutive issues as published—$17.95
TWO-YEAR SUBSCRIPTION—sixteen consecutive issues as published—$31.95
Outside U.S.A., add $6.00 per subscription year for postage and handling.

ACKNOWLEDGMENTS

ST. VALENTINE'S DAY by Edgar A. Guest from *THE PATH TO HOME.* Used by permission; SPECIAL FRIENDS from *THE STORY OF MY LIFE,* by Helen Keller, Copyright, 1903, by Helen Keller. Published by Doubleday; HEART AND HEAD by Patience Strong from *ROSES FOR RE-MEMBRANCE,* Copyright © 1960 by Patience Strong. Used by permission of Rupert Crew Literary Representa-tion, London, England. Our sincere thanks to the following whose addresses we were unable to locate: J.M. Lenahan for PEACE from the *DAVIS ANTHOLOGY OF NEWS-PAPER VERSE FOR 1933;* Mabel Ielene Rathmann for SILENT SNOWFLAKES.

Front and back covers by Al Riccio

Inside front cover by Fred Sieb

Inside back cover from H. Armstrong Roberts, Inc.

A Day of Ice

Verna Sparks

The earth is framed in ice today;
The boughs beam crystal clear.
The cedars droop from weight of ice;
Snow-capped, posts disappear.

The winter storm has wedged us in;
We watch the snowflakes fall.
It isn't long until the earth
Is not the same at all.

The junipers are humpbacked
With snow and icy pillows.
The tall pine branches look forlorn;
So do the pussy willows.

There's not a hint of breeze today—
No sun, just winter, still;
No sign of bird, no stir of wing—
Icebound, we feel the chill.

The sky is dark with heavy clouds;
Winter is here, we say.
We wrap up snug and thank the Lord
For a good warm place to stay.

Photo Opposite
WATCHTOWER AT DESERT VIEW
GRAND CANYON
Ed Cooper

Poem for a Music Box

A delicate mixture of music and art,
Delighting the eye and ear,
As round and round you turn your charms—
Your world a tinkling sphere.

Music is your heartbeat
And although its play is not long,
You make the most of your one desire—
To please with beauty and song.

Carol Baldwin
Peabody, MA

Best Friends

Your friendship means so much to me,
God blessed the day we met;
I hope that we will always be
As close as friends can get.

Your smile can brighten up my days,
You listen to my woes;
You show me in so many ways
What a special friend I chose.

I know in you I can confide
My deepest thoughts and fears.
Together we have laughed and cried;
We share both smiles and tears.

As months and years will pass us by,
I hope that we can be
Best friends forever, you and I;
You are a joy to me.

Kathy A. Schaeffer
Sunbury, PA

Reflections

New Sled

The sled rushes swiftly through the snow,
    cracking the crust and sending
        showers of stars up into the bitter
        sky.

I fly—I soar—I *zoom* down the hill,
    taking my life in my mittened hands.

My heart pounds wildly and strongly—
    a surge of excitement shortens my
        breath
        as the fence at the bottom of the hill
            rushes to meet me with splin-
            tered and ice-ridden arms.

My feet thump off the sled and
    crash through the crusty snow,
        digging into the frozen dirt and grass.

Stopped now, I smell the stinging wind,
    I feel the chapped redness creep into
        my cheeks.

Exhilarated, I look behind me at the
    small be-coated bundle
        standing at the top of the hill.

A small clear voice
    falls down the hill and catches up with
        me:
        "Mommy, can I try it now?"

Lisa Hefner Heitz
Topeka, KA

The Wonder of Woollies

Perhaps the snow is so appealing,
'Cause winter clothes are not revealing.
Fuzzy coats you get to wear
And warm wool hats to hide your hair.

Not so fit or not so thin?
Layers of wool will hide who's in
The big down coat and fur earmuffs.
Your smiling face will be enough

To show the world you're shaped okay.
It's just so very cold today.

Patricia Hershey
Santa Barbara, CA

Winter Sunrise

E. L.

It seems to me that sunrise differs
When winter's chill begins to enfold;
Her brilliant colors of scarlet reds
Are changed to all the softer golds.

For frost has squeezed the color
From the bluest of summer skies,
And made the dawn a washed-out red;
The background for a rosy sigh.

Oh, a winter sunrise brings with it
A tiny hint: its pastel shade
Is but a faint reminder
Of the riotous splendor summer made.

Perhaps someday an ingenious artist
Will capture winter's sunrise hues
And set there on an empty canvas
Pinks and ochers, then pale blues.

And so, when frosted air has come,
I quietly stand outside to stare,
And wonder at the sunrise that
The Master has subtly painted there.

Photo Opposite
LOWER KLAMATH NATIONAL
WILDLIFE REFUGE, OREGON
Grant Heilman

Magic Catalog

Joy Belle Burgess

How nice to have a catalog
On this cold and blustery night;
The magic of its pages
Fills my heart with sweet delight.

For while the back log crackles
And glowing flames leap high,
I still may go where fancy leads
Down flowering paths 'neath summer skies;

And linger there amid the blooms
Of bright and sunny marigolds,
And rainbow hues of tall larkspurs
Where velvet petals now unfold.

Then I must pause where pansies grow
And lift their faces to the sun
To feel the joy and rapture
Of this hour before my dream is done.

Thank you for this catalog,
Its pages bright and gay,
For its spell of sweet enchantment
Has unveiled a lovely summer day!

Photo Opposite
SEED CATALOG
Ralph Luedtke

COLLECTOR'S CORNER

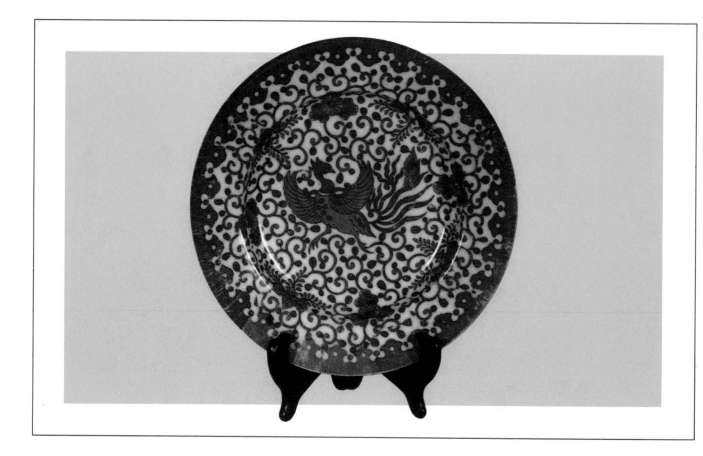

*I*n Japan, the mythical phoenix is known as Ho-o and is held sacred as an emblem of wise and good government, a symbol of good fortune, and a harbinger of happiness. Usually accompanying the phoenix are two designs: the chrysanthemum (kiku), and a three-leaf motif and its blossoms (kiri). While this mythical bird has been depicted on fabric and china for centuries, it is the twentieth-century dinnerware pattern called Phoenix Bird Chinaware which draws the attention of collectors today.

The first known advertisement for this pattern dates back to 1916. At that time it was known as "Howo Chinaware." By the mid-1920s, "Blue Howo Bird China" was being offered in sets as well as single pieces, and prices were quite low. Later, in the late 1920s and 1930s, the pieces were offered as premium gifts for grocery store purchases.

Over 500 shapes and sizes exist in the Phoenix Bird pattern. Among the more rare are a cracker trough, a cruet set in a boat-shaped holder, a covered soap dish (complete with drain), and an octagonal straight-handled coffee pot. In addition, several of the standard chinaware categories have a number of variations; for example, there are as many as fifty variations of sugar bowls and creamers, and sixteen variations of salt and pepper shakers.

A number of differences can also be found in

relation to size, quality, and color. The chinaware ranges from eggshell-thin to restaurant-thick, with the thinner being of better quality. The shades of blue vary from light blue to deep cobalt.

In 1936, England's Myott & Son copied the Phoenix Bird pattern, marking most of its pieces "Satsuma." These seem to have been for export only as those catalogued to date have all been found in the United States. These pieces differ from the Phoenix Bird in that they are earthenware, whereas the Phoenix Bird Chinaware is porcelain.

There are over ninety makers' marks for the pattern's many varied shapes and sizes from Nippon (1891-1921) to those of the Morimura Brothers: a concave "M" inside a wreath, and a convex "M" inside two crossed stems. The most common mark, however, is simply "Made in Japan."

In the early 1970s, a small number of more modern shapes began to appear in the Phoenix Bird design. They are easily distinguished from the older pieces by a harsher blue tone, a perfected pattern, and a whiter background. In addition, they were marked only with a removable sticker reading "Japan" instead of an engraved marking. These pieces do not command the prices of the older work.

Phoenix Bird Chinaware, long appreciated for its color and designs, has grown in popularity as a collectible since the 1960s. As the demand for pieces has escalated, so has the price, and pieces have become more difficult to find. Happy are the collectors who keep on tracking the Phoenix Bird: elusive, but fun to hunt!

Joan C. Oates

Joan C. Oates began rescuing Phoenix Birds when she received a small breakfast set from an aunt in 1975. Since then, she has become a noted collector of Howo Chinaware, having published three books on the subject. She also publishes a regular newsletter, Phoenix Bird Discoveries.

Photo Overleaf
WILD HORSES
Fred Sieb

Memory Time

Ruth B. Field

Clock loudly ticking away wintertime:

Wintertime — memory time; now hearts remember
Other long evenings of years we have known:
The sweet scent of roses in life's young December,
The laughter and music from years that have flown;
Children, and dreaming, and warm arms enfolding,
Moments when time stopped to heartbeats of joy,
Eyes brimmed with starlight from visions beholding,
Hours of happiness, a child with his toy;
Long winter evenings with no time to measure,
Loved ones with whom we share warmth and our dreams,
Now like a rose bowl so fondly treasured,
Its fragrance still mingled with bright fire gleams.

Ruddy, the fire burns, warmth deeply flowing.
Memories come tiptoeing over the snow.
Silhouettes nestling; heart embers blowing;
Bringing back scenes from long winters ago.

Photo Opposite
COMFORT AND WARMTH
Gerald Koser

What Is Love?

Stella Craft Tremble

Love is a cloak on a windy day. It is silks and music and perfume. It is waltzing to the "Blue Danube."

But it is also bread and meat, and dreams with raggedy edges and patched holes. It is the tear of forgiveness in the eye.

Love is hope on a dark February day; it is the echo of a carillon, an amulet worn against the ghosts of age and fear. Love is joy shared with sorrow; it is climbing on a steep incline—taking a sure step above a yawning chasm.

Love is sharing a moldy crust, the autumn mood of petals falling on a frosty hill. It is the smile hiding the tear; the arm stretched out to catch the halo falling from a cloud. Love is a flickering flame flooding the heavy air, blown by the gale, but refusing to die out.

Love is a dive for pearls in dark depths. Love is faith—meeting tragedy with calm and fortitude. Love is turning the other cheek, but it is also the double rainbow after the storm. Love is a gusty wave that flings memories on the spirit's shore; love ties these remembrances with rose-ribbons of emotion . . .

Love is the gleam of truth leading away from phantom foxfires floating in the dark. It is the soul mounting above the somber mists of greed and fear, rising to higher realms, helping to bring to earth the New Jerusalem. Love selects the dream instead of bread; the bread is devoured, but the dream lives on!

Love is the singing of wild canaries on every bough, to blend the past and future into now.

Love is finding God and losing night . . . and dwelling on the blessed peaks of light!

Photo Opposite
PASTEL BEAUTY
H. Armstrong Roberts, Inc.

The Mailman

Carice Williams

I'm glad to see our mailman call
With letters in his hand,
To bring a greeting from a friend
Who's in a far-off land.

I anxiously await his call
And hurry to the door
For sweet surprises from his pack
Sent from a foreign shore.

I think he knows the joy he brings
Whenever he comes here,
Especially when he holds a note
From someone very dear.

To My Love

Loise Pinkerton Fritz

Into my time-worn mailbox
I placed a heart-shaped card—
A valentine with lacy trim
Addressed to one afar.

It carried a meaningful poem,
Sealed with a grateful heart,
Over snow-covered hills and valleys
Its message to impart.

By way of my time-worn mailbox,
Within this wintry month,
I sent to my lover,
So distant and true,
My love for all that he's done.

Materials Needed:

Illustration of your choice

Clear acrylic spray

Cuticle scissors with short, curved blades

Piece of wood in dimensions appropriate to
   illustration

Latex paint *or* wood stain (semitransparent
   oil stain)

Brush

Sandpaper

Clean cloth

Glue

Damp sponge *or* cloth

Low luster and high gloss varnish

#280 sandpaper

#400 sandpaper

Linseed oil

Pumice powder

Felt pad

Sponge

Soft cloth

Note: Try to decoupage in as dust free an area
   as possible

Step One: Selecting Article to Decoupage

Decoupage can be used to decorate a piece of furniture or to preserve an appealing illustration on a background of wood.

Keeping in mind the dimensions of the piece to be decoupaged, choose an appropriate print. You may wish to combine two or more illustrations to create your picture.

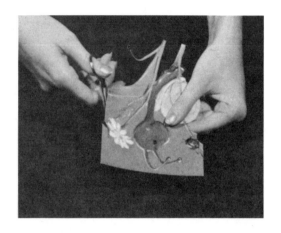

Step Two: Preparing and Cutting Out Your Print

Spray the front of your print with a light coat of acrylic spray. Allow to dry. Repeat.

To give your print a three-dimensional effect and prevent color on the underside from showing at the edges, use cuticle scissors to cut out the print. Hold the scissors with the curved blades pointing away from you while cutting.

Step Three: Preparing the Surface of Raw Wood

If using latex paint, seal raw wood with a coat of acrylic spray. Allow to dry, then brush on one coat of paint.

If staining wood, wipe on a coat of semitransparent stain and allow to dry for forty minutes. Seal with a coat of acrylic spray.

Another option is to seal the wood without painting or staining.

Lightly sand the surface until smooth. Remove sanding residue with a clean cloth.

Photo Opposite
DECORATIVE DECOUPAGE
Ralph Luedtke

Step Four: Applying the Cutout

Arrange the cutout on the prepared surface to determine positioning.

When applying a design over sections that will open or come apart (lids, doors, etc.), apply the design in one whole piece and then slit the cutout with a razor blade at the seam after the glue is dry.

Brush a thin coat of glue on the back of all pieces and carefully place on the surface.

If you are using a fragile print, brush the wood surface with glue and then position the cutout on the surface.

Wipe the print with a damp sponge or cloth, working from the center to the edge to eliminate air bubbles and pick up excess glue from the surface before varnishing. Any dried glue will be apparent in your finished work.

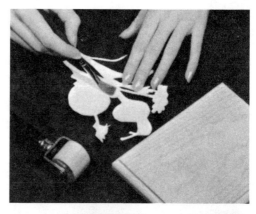

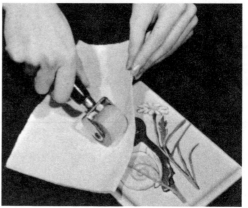

Step Five: Varnishing

A minimum of twenty coats of varnish is recommended for surfaces with applied designs. Always allow twenty-four hours of drying time between each coat of varnish and no more than forty-eight hours between each of the first ten coats. Any longer time lapse between coats at this time will necessitate light sanding which could damage your print before you have the initial ten-coat buildup.

Use low luster varnish for the first two coats. Follow with eight coats of high gloss varnish.

After the initial ten coats have been applied, sand the surface with a wet piece of #280 sandpaper.

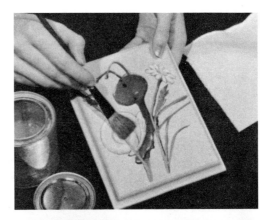

Apply five coats of high gloss varnish, sanding between each coat with wet #400 sandpaper.

If you wish to use a total of more than twenty coats of varnish, you will want to apply them at this time. The number of coats of varnish you may apply is unlimited; the more coats used, the greater the dimensional effect. The final five coats, however, should always be of low luster varnish.

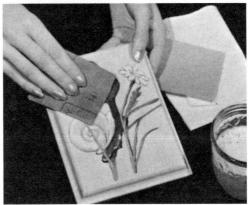

For the final low luster finishing, apply three coats of low luster varnish, then sand with wet #400 sandpaper. Apply the final two coats of low luster varnish. If you exceed twenty-four hours drying time between coats, sand lightly before applying the next coat of varnish to assure good adhesion.

Step Six: Finishing

Mix two tablespoons of linseed oil with two tablespoons of pumice powder. Using a felt pad dipped in the pumice-oil mixture, rub the surface in one direction, exerting some pressure but not enough to rub through the low luster varnish into the gloss.

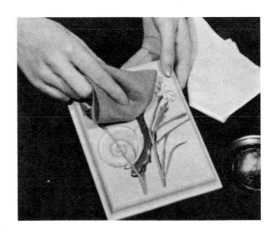

Sponge the surface with soap and water. Rinse and dry thoroughly.

Polish with a clean soft cloth.

Love of Poetry

Craig E. Sathoff

"I have no love of poetry,"
I heard a fellow say,
"For it is frivolous and trite
And wastes the time of day."

I could not help but disagree,
For countless times each day
I feel the joy of poetry
That gently holds its sway.

The poetry of Psalms and Ruth
Is soothing to my heart
With wisdom, peace, and guidance
That its messages impart.

The nursery rhymes I read my
  young,
The church hymns that I sing,
The tunes I hum while fast at work
All have poetic ring.

For when the heart is filled with joy,
It lends itself to song,
And life is filled with poetry
As moments rush along.

And when the heart is void of
  cheer,
And little hope shines through,
The gentle calm of poetry
Can be a comfort, too.

I feel the power of poetry
Within my every day.
I thrill to hear its glad refrain
As I go on my way.

Photo Opposite
TAPESTRY AND CANE
Peter Neumann
The Stock Market

Wall design courtesy of
ICI Wallcoverings

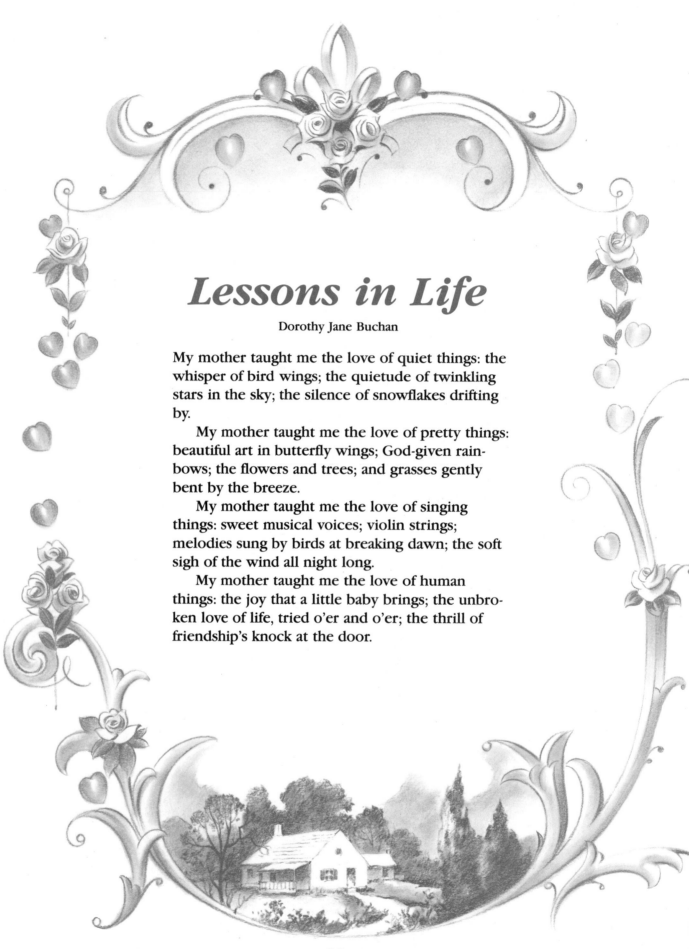

Lessons in Life

Dorothy Jane Buchan

My mother taught me the love of quiet things: the whisper of bird wings; the quietude of twinkling stars in the sky; the silence of snowflakes drifting by.

My mother taught me the love of pretty things: beautiful art in butterfly wings; God-given rainbows; the flowers and trees; and grasses gently bent by the breeze.

My mother taught me the love of singing things: sweet musical voices; violin strings; melodies sung by birds at breaking dawn; the soft sigh of the wind all night long.

My mother taught me the love of human things: the joy that a little baby brings; the unbroken love of life, tried o'er and o'er; the thrill of friendship's knock at the door.

Special Friends

Helen Keller

Those are red-letter days in our lives when we meet people who thrill us like a fine poem, people whose handshakes are brimful of unspoken sympathy and whose sweet, rich natures impart to our eager, impatient spirits a wonderful restlessness which, in its essence, is divine.

The perplexities, irritations, and worries that have absorbed us pass like unpleasant dreams, and we wake to see with new eyes and hear with new ears the beauty and harmony of God's real world. The solemn nothings that fill our everyday life blossom suddenly into bright possibilities.

In a word, while such friends are near us, we feel that all is well. Perhaps we never saw them before and they may never cross our life's path again; but the influence of their calm, mellow natures is a libation poured upon our discontent, and we feel its healing touch as the ocean feels the mountain stream freshening its brine.

Hopelessly Romantic

Nadine Gardner

Are we hopelessly romantic,
Just two sentimental fools?
Well, according to our modern friends,
We're breaking all the rules.
Still adoring lighted candles
On the table while we dine;
We've never lost our preference for
Those songs from '49.

On sunny days in August,
On a picnic by the stream,
We sit for endless hours
Sharing secret hopes and dreams.
On starry nights in April,
You and I walk hand in hand
To that bridge where, thirty years ago,
Our wedding day we planned.

In my personal opinion
Hopeless fools we never were;
Though some may still maintain the thought,
They're wrong, of that I'm sure.
But, yes, we're sentimental,
Quite romantically inclined,
And in my heart you'll always be
My favorite valentine.

28

The Healing of the Heart

Joan Wester Anderson

Here I sit, surrounded by my mending chores. There's the torn ear on the baby's much-loved plush panda which must be secured again so it can endure another hug. There are buttons to sew on the boys' shirts, hems to let down for the daughter growing far too quickly, patches needed for the teenager's work pants. I have never been very good at sewing, but I keep trying—for this is part of a mother's role.

My husband has his own repair jobs to do. The workbench is littered with little wheels that must be soldered onto racing cars. There's a beloved doll with an arm to be readjusted and a new pair of pedals for the fifth grader's bike. My husband is not a mechanical genius. But the children have faith in him; and he has learned to be worthy of that faith.

We parents do a lot of fixing. Sometimes we know just where the glue should go, just how hard to turn the screwdriver, and the broken piece becomes magically whole again. But there are some repair jobs that challenge our abilities to the fullest and make us wonder if we will ever succeed. These are the mending jobs we do on the children themselves.

It's easy, of course, to fix the injured dignity of the toddler who falls as he runs to greet me. Just a hug, a light dusting and he is off again, pride restored. But what does one do when it is the ten-year-old who trips—on his way to catch the last fly ball with a crowd of Little League families all watching? His father and I feel his humiliation across the field—but there isn't a bandage big enough to soothe the ache.

And what of the child who is struggling to master the multiplication tables, the son who feels friendless and lonely, the daughter who wasn't asked to a party, the married offspring whose tense, tight-lipped face signals a problem he cannot discuss? How do we repair their shattered spirits and restore their belief in themselves? There are no directions for jobs like these, no printed patterns for parents to follow.

And so, hesitant and inept, we mend with the only materials available to us, our hearts. We hold our children close, feeling their disappointments, calming their fears. We leave a little note under someone's pillow, bake a favorite dessert. Wordlessly, we touch a cheek, refusing to belittle grief with a blustery pep talk, choosing instead to silently share. And gradually our children grow to understand that, rather than being alone, they can heal with our gentle touch of love.

It is all we can do, the only way we know. Yet, through the years, God teaches us that it is his way, too, and it is enough. For in this job of family mending, there is a time for everything. A time to rock and hug, and a time to laugh the hurt away. A time to walk and talk together, and a time to sit quietly, comforting in silence. A time to take action, and a time to leave the healing in His hands. And however inadequate we feel, there is always time for love.

Needles and thread, pliers and nails will fix our children's belongings. But love is the glue that mends their broken hearts.

LOVE

Anonymous

I love you,
Not only for what you are,
But for what I am
When I am with you.

I love you,
Not only for what
You have made of yourself,
But for what
You are making of me.

I love you
For the part of me
That you bring out;
I love you
For putting your hand
Into my heaped-up heart
And passing over
All the foolish, weak things
That you can't help
Dimly seeing there,
And for drawing out
Into the light
All the beautiful belongings
That no one else had looked
Quite far enough to find.

I love you because you
Are helping me to make
Of the lumber of my life
Not a tavern,
But a temple;
Out of the works
Of my every day
Not a reproach,
But a song . . .

Little Things

Pamela Kennedy

I was talking the other day with a friend. She has been married a year or so—long enough to realize the honeymoon is over, I guess you'd say.

"You know," she said, sighing, "it just isn't like I thought it would be."

I stirred my tea and glanced at her. "And how was that?" I asked.

"Oh, romantic, you know." She looked wistful and went on. "I'd love to have him bring me flowers as a surprise now and then or whisk me off for a romantic weekend someplace. You know, the things that keep a marriage exciting."

I nodded, smiling, thinking back over the twenty years of my marriage. It still seemed romantic to me, but it wasn't because of flowers and getaway weekends. There were little things, simple things, that kept the romance real.

A phone call on a weekday afternoon kept me going when I felt unappreciated. The children's needs and schedules filled my hours to overflowing, and the laundry seemed to multiply before my eyes; then he called and said, "I think you're wonderful." Those few words changed my outlook, made my labor one of love, and replaced my complaints with song. Such a simple thing really.

Then there was the basket of strawberries, plump and red as rubies sparkling in the sun. It was Mother's Day and all the moms I knew got flowers—all but me.

"I looked at roses," he said with love in his eyes, "but I brought you these instead." He remembered the child in me, sticky sweet in the dust of a sun-warmed berry patch, juice dripping from crimson fingers. No basket of berries was ever more cherished than those.

How many small but important sacrifices over the past two decades had reinforced my knowledge of his love for me? I recall my husband passing up a long-awaited golf outing to help with a sick child. On several occasions, he took time out from his busy work schedule to play house-husband while I attended a special class or conference. One year he suggested that we spend our vacation visiting my favorite relatives when he would have much preferred to spend it in a quiet mountain cabin with just me. The everyday give-and-take of a growing relationship became the currency of our romance.

But romance doesn't consist of only bright and shining moments. The fabric of love has its darker shades as well. Interwoven with the joys and blessings were the difficulties we had faced together—sleepless nights spent with feverish babies, job transfers to places to which we didn't want to go, anxious hours spent waiting for medical diagnoses, losses, even death. Yet, as we clung together through these times, the love and romance grew and our relationship grew with them, stronger and more resilient than before.

But how could I tell all this to a disappointed bride who waited breathlessly for bouquets? Her concerns were honest, but only time would help her understand the reality of romance.

"Just wait," I said finally, with a reassuring smile. "Romance has a way of finding its way into a relationship in a variety of unexpected ways. It takes time, though, and lots of little things to make a romance real."

Pamela Kennedy is a freelance writer of short stories, articles, essays, and children's books. Married to a naval officer and mother of three children, she has made her home on both U.S. coasts and currently resides in Hawaii. She draws her material from her own experiences and memories, adding bits of imagination to create a story or mood.

Photo Overleaf
ARTISTRY IN ICE
LAKE SUPERIOR
Ken Dequaine

A Slice of Life

Edgar A. Guest

Let loose the sails of love and let them fill
    With breezes sweet with tenderness today;
    Scorn not the praises youthful lovers say;
Romance is old, but it is lovely still.
    Not he who shows his love deserves the jeer,
    But he who speaks not what she longs to hear.
There is no shame in love's devoted speech;
    Man need not blush his tenderness to show.
    'Tis shame to love and never let her know,
To keep his heart forever out of reach.
    Not he the fool who lets his love go on,
    But he who spurns it when his love is won.
Men proudly vaunt their love of gold and fame,
    High station and accomplishments of skill,
    Yet of life's greatest conquest they are still,
And deem it weakness, or an act of shame
    To seem to place high value on the love
    Which first of all they should be proudest of.
Let loose the sails of love and let them take
    The tender breezes till the day be spent;
    Only the fool chokes out life's sentiment.
She is a prize too lovely to forsake.
    Be not ashamed to send your valentine;
    She has your love, but needs its outward sign.

The Passionate Shepherd to His Love

Christopher Marlowe

Come live with me and be my Love,
And we will all the pleasures prove
That hills and valleys, dale and field,
And all the craggy mountains yield.

There will we sit upon the rocks
And see the shepherds feed their flocks,
By shallow rivers, to whose falls
Melodious birds sing madrigals.

There will I make thee beds of roses
And a thousand fragrant posies,
A cap of flowers, and a kirtle
Embroider'd all with leaves of myrtle.

A gown made of the finest wool,
Which from our pretty lambs we pull,
Fair linéd slippers for the cold,
With buckles of the purest gold.

A belt of straw and ivy buds
With coral clasps and amber studs:
And if these pleasures may thee move,
Come live with me and be my Love.

Thy silver dishes for thy meat
As precious as the gods do eat,
Shall on an ivory table be
Prepared each day for thee and me.

The shepherd swains shall dance and sing
For thy delight each May morning:
If these delights thy mind may move,
Then live with me and be my Love.

Photo Opposite
HEARTS AND FLOWERS
Al Riccio

Hand in Hand

Phyllis C. Michael

Hand in hand may you find joy,
True joy beyond all measure;
Hand in hand may you create
Fond memories to treasure.

Hand in hand, as time goes by,
May love grow even stronger —
Hand in hand, year after year,
Though paths seem steeper, longer.

Hand in hand with faith and hope
May you walk close together —
Hand in hand as each day dawns
Regardless of the weather.

Hand in hand may you fulfill
Your every secret longing.
Hand in hand may you each know
The comfort of belonging.

Hand in hand may God guide you,
His grace, his love possessing.
Hand in hand may he grant you
His most abundant blessing.

Heart or Head

Patience Strong

My heart is saying — This is love.
But can it really be?
My heart is saying — This is it.
It says you're meant for me . . .
But how, I wonder, can I tell
If this is truly so?
Can the wayward heart be trusted?
How am I to know?

Common sense says — Wait awhile.
Don't risk a big mistake.
Pause before you start to think
About a wedding cake . . .
Look before you take a final
Leap into the blue.
But my heart says, "Fiddlesticks!"
So what am I to do?

I admit that in the past
I've often been misled —
But now it comes to this: am I
To follow heart or head?
I ought to heed the voice that says
It can't be genuine;
And yet I have a feeling that
My heart is going to win.

In Snow Time

Sidney Lanier

How should I choose to walk the world with thee,
Mine own beloved? When green grass is stirred
By summer breezes, and each leafy tree
Shelters the nest of many a singing bird?
To walk with thee along a wintry road,
Through flowerless fields, thick-sown with frosty rime,
Beside an ice-bound stream, whose waters flowed
In voiceless music all the summertime?
In winter dreariness, or summer glee?
How shall I choose to walk the world with thee?

The time of roses is the time of love,
Ah! my dear heart! but winter fires are bright,
And in the lack of sunshine from above
We tend more carefully love's sacred light.
The path among the roses lieth soft,
Sun-kissed and radiant under youthful feet;
But on a wintry day true hands more oft
Do meet and cling in pressure close and sweet.
Let others share thy life's glad summer glow,
But let me walk beside thee in its snow.

Photo Opposite
A WALK IN SNOW
Tom Grill
Comstock

Down Life's Stream

Margaret Sangster

A bride and groom were spending their honeymoon in the loveliness of the country—watching all of the world stretch out wide and sun-filled and wonderful before them.

Because they were modern, athletic young people, they thought that it would be more splendid to have the sort of a honeymoon that would be filled with the glow of the outdoors. But many of the bride's friends told her that she was foolish.

"Go to a great city," they told her, "where you can have the excitement of crowds to remember, and the thrill of big hotels, and the fun of music and laughter and shops. Life is so quiet—it settles down to such humdrum things—after the honeymoon is over. Maybe you'll never have a chance to get away again!"

The bride repeated all of this to the groom—and her smile was very sweet as she did.

"As if," she said, "we will ever settle down to humdrum things after we have come back from the honeymoon! Why, we couldn't! Because we love each other!"

The groom kissed her. It was his reply.

And so they started out, with plenty of flannel shirts and rubber-soled shoes. And they kept far away from the great cities and the shops and the crowds. But they didn't lack for music and laughter. For they laughed together over all of the small, amusing happenings of every day. And their hearts made the most glorious music that was ever written!

One day they were paddling down a quiet stream in a slim canoe. The water rippled about their craft as they went. And the shafts of sunlight made a green-gold color all about them. And suddenly the groom spoke.

"I wonder," he said, "why folks are always saying such things? The sort of things that your friends said, when you told them our plans for a honeymoon! Why do people talk as if marriage were a prison? Why can't it always be as lovely as it is now?"

The bride stopped paddling. Her pretty face was very thoughtful as she answered.

"Of course, I don't agree with people who say such things," she answered at last, speaking slowly. "Of course, feeling as I do, about you and our years-to-be, *I can't agree with them!* But it's true, regrettably so, that I do see people all about who do settle down after marriage. Who don't get away. Who view life through bars. The bars," she laughed, ever so ruefully, "of habit!"

The groom spoke again.

"But it isn't necessary—" he began.

The bride interrupted.

"It isn't necessary that loveliness should

ever cease," she said, "not even if a marriage is a hundred years old! Marriage, if it is handled in the right way, should be as beautiful as drifting down a stream. In fact," she paused . . .

"The fun about all of this," she continued, and a gesture of her round young arm took in the sparkling water and the trees and the sunlight, "is the prettiness and the unexpectedness of it. We never know just what we're going to see when we turn a curve in the stream. We never know just when a bird is going to sing for us from some overhanging branch. We never know when a cardinal flower is going to lend a splash of scarlet to the bank. We never know exactly . . . "

It was the groom's turn to interrupt.

"Also," he mentioned, "we never know when the canoe may hit a rock and turn over. When it may be caught in rapids. When a storm may sweep over the sky. All the things that may happen to us aren't pleasantry."

Quite seriously the bride surveyed the groom.

"I'm ashamed of you!" she said. "You shouldn't have brought that up! Of course we know that there are hidden rocks and rapids and storms. But we don't let it take the sunshine from this day, do we? Of course we know that in life there are pitfalls and troubles. But wasn't that all covered by the words of the marriage ceremony? 'For better, for worse,'" she quoted, " 'In sickness and in health.' "

"I apologize!" the groom laughed. "I apologize to you, little champion of marriage!"

The bride joined in his laughter.

"And I accept your apology!" she told him. "But, always remember this. The trouble with most marriages is just the sort of thing that you've mentioned. The looking forward, around the bend in the stream, to the hidden rock and the treacherous current, rather than the expecting of a bird song or a gay flower. The looking ahead, in expectation of storms, rather than expecting to look ahead and see lovely weather. It's awfully easy to take the romance out of marriage, to make marriage humdrum—just as they all told me! But I," proudly the bride's little chin was lifting, "I'm never going to allow myself to talk me out of the beauty of living! I know that there will be troubles and illness and—yes, squabbles. We're human . . . But I'm always going to keep them in their proper place. In a place that's less important than the fact that we love each other and are going to keep right on loving each other."

The groom was speaking.

"The sunlight on your hair," he said, "it's the prettiest thing I ever saw! Say," his voice was boyishly eager, "if you keep your paddle very steady I'd be able to come forward far enough to kiss you—without capsizing the canoe."

And the bride held her paddle very steady, indeed!

Treasured Valentine

LaVerne P. Larson

I'll see those fancy valentines
For sale in every store;
Yet there's a very special kind
I always treasure more.

The printed ones are nice, of course,
With verse and lace and such;
But somehow they just seem to lack
That warm and loving touch.

The valentine I treasure most
Is given with a kiss
And fashioned by dear little hands
To fill my heart with bliss.

It's given with a joyful hug;
And though I shed a tear,
It fills my heart with happiness
The same way every year.

Too soon those busy little hands
Will buy one at the store;
And yet my heart will treasure most
The valentines of yore.

Photo Opposite
A VALENTINE OF LOVE
Dietrich Photography

My Two Valentines

LaVerne P. Larson

I have two lovely valentines
Each day of every year—
A smiling lass, a smiling lad
Whom I hold very dear.

Their little hearts hold so much love
And sing with joy untold;
And I am richer than a king
With love worth more than gold.

They kiss me and they hug me
And climb upon my knee;
It's good to just be living
In their happy company.

We share so many hours
Of fun and secrets, too;
It isn't any wonder
That I love them like I do.

Their laughter and their smiles,
The twinkle in their eyes
Make every day I share with them
A wonderful surprise.

Candy, cards, or flowers
Can make a person glad,
But I am truly blessed, indeed,
With my smiling lass and lad.

51

From *I'm Thankful Each Day!* by P.K. Hallinan
Published by Ideals Publishing Corp., Nashville, TN 37214.

I'm Thankful Each Day

P. K. Hallinan

I'm thankful each day
for the blessings I see
and for all of the gifts
that are given to me.

And counting the stars
at the edge of the sea,
I can't help but feel
they were put there for me.

I'm thankful for summers
and warm golden days;
I'm thankful for autumns
of orange pumpkin haze.

I'm thankful for meadows
and bright colored flowers;
I'm thankful for raindrops
and soft summer showers.

Each sunset is special;
each sunrise is new.
Each breeze in the trees
is a promise come true.

Each evening's a wonder
where beauty abounds;
each morning's a harvest
of new sights and sounds.

And it's nice just to know
that beneath winter snow
the blossoms of spring
are beginning to grow.

I'm thankful for friends,
for laughing and sharing.
I'm thankful for family,
for loving and caring.

I'm thankful for all
the kindness I see.
I'm thankful for peace
and for pure harmony.

My body's a present
of perfect design;
my mind is a power
as endless as time.

And if ever I worry
that trouble is near,
I always remember
there is nothing to fear—

for each hour is laden
with infinite love;
each second brings comfort
and joy from above.

And I guess in the end
the best thing to say
is I'm thankful for living—
I'm thankful each day!

Enchanted Day

Judith F. Pearson

The world has stopped outside our door.
The kids are home: one-two-three-four.
When snow days trap their energy,
Mom plots a way to set it free.
"Let's pretend we're all snowbound
Away from modern sights and sounds.
We'll share a day so very full
With fresh snow-cream, a taffy pull?
And popcorn crisp, beside the fire,
Whatever games you each desire."
Then outside, there's a fort to build,
With angels bright the lawn is filled,
A game of fox and geese is laid,
Mom's energy begins to fade!
It's back inside to warm our toes,
With cocoa hot, sweet marshmallows.
The neighbor crew drops by to see
Why this dull day we spend with glee.
"We're snowbound here!" we cry aloud.
"Come on in and join the crowd.
Our mom has stopped the world today,
On this enchanted holiday!"

Pirouettes

Makes 30 to 36

½ cup butter, softened
½ cup granulated sugar
1 teaspoon vanilla
2 egg whites
⅔ cup flour
Chocolate Filling

Preheat oven to 375°. Cream butter, sugar, and vanilla in bowl until fluffy; beat in egg whites. Stir in flour just until blended. Drop by teaspoonfuls 3 inches apart on baking sheet. Spread with back of a wet spoon to 3-inch circles. Bake on middle oven rack 5 minutes or until edges are light brown. Loosen 1 cookie at a time from baking sheet with spatula. Working quickly, turn over and roll tightly around a pencil. Cool seam-side-down on rack. Fill pirouettes with Chocolate Filling using pastry bag, or frost insides with wooden pick or soda straw.

Chocolate Filling

3 ounces semisweet chocolate chips
¼ teaspoon vegetable oil, butter, *or* margarine

Melt chocolate with oil in saucepan over low heat; stir until smooth.

Viennese Fingers

Makes 24

1 cup flour
½ cup butter *or* margarine, softened
½ cup finely chopped walnuts *or* pecans
¼ cup confectioners' sugar
½ teaspoon vanilla
¼ teaspoon almond extract
Chocolate Glaze
Chocolate jimmies, nonpareils, *or* flaked coconut

Mix first 6 ingredients in bowl; shape into flat ball. Wrap in waxed paper. Chill 45 minutes. Preheat oven to 375°. Divide into 24 balls; roll each into 3-inch length, curving into crescent shape, or roll each into 2-inch length, shaping into oval. Place on baking sheet. Bake 10 minutes or until set but not brown. Let set 1 minute. Cool on rack. Prepare Chocolate Glaze; dip ends in glaze; then into jimmies, nonpareils, or flaked coconut. Chill until serving time.

Chocolate Glaze

1½ squares (1 ounce each) semisweet chocolate
1½ teaspoons light corn syrup
1½ teaspoons cream

Melt chocolate with corn syrup and cream in saucepan over low heat; stir to mix.

Baklava

Make this divine Greek pastry a day ahead.

Makes approximately 54 pieces.

21 sheets phyllo dough, thawed in wrappings
7 cups chopped walnuts
1 tablespoon ground cinnamon
½ cup granulated sugar
1½ cups butter *or* combination butter and margarine, melted
Syrup

Cut phyllo sheets in half crosswise to fit in bottom of greased 9 x 13-inch baking pan. Cover sheets with damp towel. Mix nuts, cinnamon, and sugar in bowl. Layer 9 half sheets of phyllo in pan, brushing each with melted butter. Sprinkle 1 cup nut mixture over phyllo sheets in pan; drizzle with some butter. Top with 4 half sheets, brushing each with melted butter. Sprinkle with 1 cup nuts and drizzle with butter. Repeat steps 5 more times. Top with remaining 9 half sheets of phyllo brushing each with butter. Cut into diamond shapes or squares almost through to bottom layer. Preheat oven to 325°. Bake 60 minutes. Cut completely through. Cool. Pour warm Syrup over cooled pastry. Cool.

Syrup

2 cups granulated sugar
1 cup water
¼ cup honey
2 tablespoons lemon juice
1 2-inch stick cinnamon

Bring all ingredients to boil in saucepan; reduce heat and cook 15 minutes, uncovered. Remove cinnamon stick. Stir and cool slightly.

* * *

Cookies that are to be dipped in confectioners' sugar look better if dipped twice—once when warm, again when cool.

Ideals Trivia

1. When was the first issue of *Ideals* published?
2. What one title has been published every year since the inception of *Ideals*?
3. Who was the founder of *Ideals* magazine?
4. In what city did the magazine originate?

The answers to these questions can be found in the following passage.

Ideals magazine actually began as an outgrowth of a personal hobby of its founder, Mr. Van B. Hooper, who collected beautiful poems, articles, and pictures for his own scrapbooks.

While editing a company newsletter, *The Messenger*, for a large manufacturing firm in Milwaukee, Wisconsin, Mr. Hooper would occasionally insert homey poetry, quotations, and photographs for the enjoyment of the employees.

The employees shared *The Messenger* with their families, and also began sharing it with friends and neighbors. The popularity of the newsletter grew until requests began to come in from people who were not associated with the company or even residing in the immediate area.

In December 1944, in response to many requests, Mr. Hooper published a magazine of his own. He christened it *Ideals* and filled it with poems and pictures he loved. That first issue was a Christmas issue—a title which has appeared each year since 1944.

Ideals has grown since that first issue of almost forty-five years ago; however, the underlying foundation—love of God, family, and country—remains.

The true test of a man's worth is not his theology but his life.

The Talmud

Knowledge is proud that he has learned so much; wisdom is humble that he knows no more.

Cowper

PIECES

Greater love hath no man than this, that a man lay down his life for his friends.

John 15:13

Liberty is not in any form of government. It is in the heart of free man; he carries it with him everywhere.

Rousseau

Time has no flight,—'tis we who speed along. The days and nights are but the same as when The earth awoke with the first rush of song, And felt the swiftly passing feet of men.

Thomas S. Collier

I am certain of nothing but of the holiness of the heart's affections, and the truth of Imagination. What the Imagination seizes as Beauty must be Truth.

Keats

Good temper, like a sunny day, sheds a brightness over everything; it is the sweetener of toil and the soother of disquietude.

Irving

Wedding Rings

The wedding ring, being circular, has long been a symbol of unending love—love which flows continuously from one person to another.

According to popular legend, there are three reasons for wearing the wedding ring on the third finger of the left hand.

The first is a physiological theory formulated before blood was known to circulate. The Romans, and before them the Greeks and Egyptians, spoke of the *vena amoris,* the vein of love. This vein, they determined, connected the third finger of the left hand directly with the heart. And the heart, of course, is the seat of tender feelings.

The second reason is a simple process of elimination. The thumb, the Romans declared, is too often used to be set apart; the forefinger and little finger are each exposed on one side; and the middle finger is too ostentatious. Therefore, the third finger was the only logical choice.

The third reason has its basis in the ancient marriage ceremony. As a symbol of faith in the sanctity of marriage, the bridegroom touched one finger on the bride's hand for each person in the Trinity, beginning with the thumb. Thus, he would complete the Trinity with the middle finger, then put the wedding band on the next, or third finger.

Silence At Three O'Clock

Jean Johnson

I awaken, get out of bed, and go to the window to rest my forehead against the cold glass. The snow that has started to fall again from the darkened sky is lifted up by the wind, swirled around, and finally permitted to float to the ground. The trees that were dead only a few hours before are now alive, their branches glistening in the light from the street lamps.

Silence. It's as if the world has stopped to let the snow settle undisturbed. It covers the ground with a soft, glittering blanket to lie there peacefully for a while longer before it will be marred by machines and humans.

But no humans exist outside at this hour, only clear beauty, only this pure nonhuman white. This is the time when nature speaks for those who want to listen, but only at this hour. The cold, clean air freezes all other sounds; the snow cushions them.

It is a time when I feel that only God and I are awake.

Photo Opposite
SILENT SNOW
Fred Sieb

Walled by a Book

Elinor Lennen

Walled by a book, however fierce the storm,
One need not hear the wind nor feel the cold.
Words build a shelter, adequate and warm,
Which years cannot attack nor use make old.
How many others on what other days
Sought this retreat and claimed it for a time:
Protected from life's hazards by a phrase;
Companioned by a story or a rhyme!

Men yet unborn shall seek this tried defense
When refuge fails that seemed secure and strong . . .
Shall balance losses by the recompense
Of sober truth, of stirring tale or song.
Give him no sorry sigh nor pitying look
Who has the single solace of a book!

Annable

Peace

J. M. Lenahan

A cheerful fire on a winter's night,
And a high-backed rocking chair,
The strains of music that I love
Drifting in on the winter air.

A quiet nook in a mountain glade,
The sun shut out by whispering trees,
Where a babbling brook goes laughing by
On its way to the seven seas.

A book beloved, and a trusted friend
To counsel and advise
When the chill winds of adversity
Swoop down from leaden skies.

The love of family and of friends,
The hope of a life to be,
The trust and faith of a little child,
That's what peace means to me.

True Love

William Shakespeare

Let me not to the marriage of true minds
Admit impediments. Love is not love
Which alters when it alteration finds,
Or bends with the remover to remove.

Oh, no! it is an ever-fixed mark
That looks on tempests, and is never shaken;
It is the star to every wandering bark,
Whose worth's unknown, although his height
   be taken.

Love's not Time's fool, though rosy lips and cheeks
Within his bending sickle's compass come;
Love alters not with his brief hours and weeks,
But bears it out ev'n to the edge of doom.

If this be error, and upon me proved,
I never writ, nor no man ever loved.

Photo Opposite
A SIGN OF LOVE
Al Riccio

Silent Snowflakes

Mabel Ielene Rathmann

In silence snowflakes fall
    All through the night;
The ground is covered with
    Diamonds in the soft moonlight.
Tree limbs are all trimmed
    With shimmering lace;
The countryside tonight
    Is a transformed place.

Each tiny twig has
    A trim all its own;
Such magnificent beauty
    O'er the country is known.
Fenceposts as marble statues
    Stand stiff and white
Resembling silent sentries
    On this cold, wintry night.

Nestled up snugly in a
    Spreading grove of trees,
A picturesque farmhouse
    Is protected from the breeze.
A happy, contented family
    In their cozy beds sleep
Knowing in their hearts
    Them the Lord will safely keep.

The Winter's Green

Barb O'Hara

The seasons call the leaves to fall
In windy celebration
Of changing scenes from summer
    greens
To brighter coloration.

The autumn falls to stormy squalls
Of rain in transformation;
And colors fade, now overlaid
With white accumulation.

The trees are bare in winter's air
And all is glaring lightness;
Yet standing full in needled wool
Is green against the whiteness.

With no excuse, the living spruce
Stands clothed in her unreason;
With no concern for weather's turn,
She lives for every season.

By great design, always the pine
Contrasts the changing scene;
Through fallen gold and growing cold
Warm stands the winter's green.

COUNTRY CHRONICLE

Lansing Christman

The world is transformed into a wonderland of glittering enchantment when the sun appears after a February snow. The storm has embroidered a blanket of lace on field and wood; and now sunlight scatters the jewels of winter over the earth.

In the blushing dawn of this Valentine's Day, my wife, Lucile, and I continue a sixty-year-old tradition. We pledge anew our heartfelt love that has endured through the past and continues to grow with each day. The love we share is as constant as each new sunrise over the eastern hills.

We discovered the essence of Valentine's Day

70

long ago when we walked in the springtime of life. Then we shared our dreams, facing the distant horizon together. We have kept those dreams alive, and time and memories have made them richer and more dear. Love, like a vintage nectar, sweetens with age.

And now, on this crisp and clear Valentine's Day, we walk across the pristine beauty left on our land by winter's gifted seamstress. The sun smiles down on winter's handiwork, casting shadows behind trees and walls, and creating images among hedges and along ruffling drifts.

We walk along an old country lane which fol-

lows a rippling, snow-lined brook. Overhead, the evergreens, weighted by their crystalline cover, form a graceful bower for our trek. Their branches interlock and form a whispering ring of hands. The wind strums the needles of the pines like a harpist plucking the strings in accompaniment to the ageless symphony of love.

The author of two published books, Lansing Christman has been contributing to Ideals *for almost twenty years. Mr. Christman has also been published in several American, foreign, and braille anthologies. He and his wife, Lucile, live in rural South Carolina where they enjoy the pleasures of the land around them.*

Fireside Memories

Carice Williams

My fireside could tell sweet tales
    Of memories from long ago,
When other hearts in other worlds
    Would daydream in its golden glow.

'Twould tell of children, rosy-cheeked,
    Who'd run in from their play
To warm up tiny hands and feet
    Before its crimson ray.

'Twould also tell of lovers, fair,
    With dreams and hopes as high
And bright as any brilliant flame
    That softly dances by.

The memories my fireside holds,
    Though dimmed sometimes by tears,
Are souvenirs I cherish most
    Through every passing year.

Photo Opposite
FIRESIDE WARMTH
Ralph Luedtke

London Snow

Robert Bridges

When men were all asleep, the snow came flying,
In large white flakes falling on the city brown,
Stealthily and perpetually settling and loosely lying,
    Hushing the latest traffic of the drowsy town;
Deadening, muffling, stifling, its murmurs failing;
Lazily and incessantly floating down and down:
    Silently sifting and veiling road, roof, and railing;
Hiding difference, making unevenness even,
Into angles and crevices softly drifting and sailing.
    All night it fell, and when full inches seven
It lay in the depth of its uncompacted lightness,
The clouds blew off from a high and frosty heaven;
    And all woke earlier for the unaccustomed brightness
Of the winter dawning, the strange unheavenly glare:
The eye marvelled—marvelled at the dazzling whiteness;
    The ear harkened to the stillness of the solemn air;
No sound of wheel rumbling nor of foot falling,
And the busy morning cries came thin and spare.
    The boys I heard, as they went to school, calling,
They gathered up the crystal manna to freeze
Their tongues with tasting, their hands with snowballing;
    Or rioted in a drift, plunging up to the knees;
Or peering up from under the white-mossed wonder,
"Oh, look at the trees!" they cried, "Oh, look at the trees!"
    With lessened load a few carts creak and blunder,
Following along the white deserted way,
A country company long dispersed asunder:
    When now already the sun, in pale display
Standing by Paul's* high dome, spread forth below
His sparkling beams, and awoke the stir of the day.
    For now doors open, and war is waged with the snow;
And trains of somber men, past tale of number,
Tread long brown paths, as toward their toil they go:
    But even for them awhile no cares encumber
Their minds diverted; the daily word is unspoken,
The daily thoughts of labor and sorrow slumber
At the sight of the beauty that greets them, for the charm
        they have broken.

*Refers to St. Paul's Cathedral in Central London

Pototschnik

78

Winter Magic

Charlene Bowen

Microscopic pearls of moisture
Rise to meet the frosty air,
Each particle of mist transformed
To crystal while suspended there.
Drops of silver caught and held,
Transfigured by some magic feat
Until each one becomes a star,
The metamorphosis complete.

Then each complete and perfect snowflake
Fashioned by the Master's hand
Descends and settles here below
To make the earth a fairyland
That glitters with a million gems
Of radiant and subtle hue,
To melt and soar again on high—
The cycle thus begins anew.

Readers' Forum

I have received the Ideals *magazine for a number of years and use it quite often for devotions and readings for various organizations. I look forward to each and every issue.*

Mrs. Joyce M. Schreiber
Williamsburg, Iowa

My thanks to each and every one on the staff of Ideals *for the most outstanding periodical of its kind. It shall truly become a treasured collection of readings for me.*

Mrs. Malia McCauley
Prescott, Arizona

I do enjoy Ideals *and look forward to many more issues. The photos are beautiful! I travel the country through* Ideals.

Mrs. Hattie M. Lever
Anderson, South Carolina

Thank you for the beautiful editions of Ideals. *The poems, pictures, and readings are so refreshing, like a cool drink of water when we are thirsty.*

Orpha R. Santa
Duluth, Minnesota

I wait eagerly for each issue and I am never disappointed with the lovely, inspirational writings, and the pictures fill me with beautiful thoughts of the present and the past.

Mrs. Lloyd Fredrickson
Brookins, South Dakota

Ideals *is a magazine that you don't throw away. You pass it around so others can enjoy it also and then you file it for future enjoyment.*

Janice Mielke
Vineland, New Jersey

As an educator, I must compliment Ideals. *Every issue is perfection. Poetry, stories, and photography create one of the most rewarding publications available. I love it!*

Claire Pfeffer
Lexington, Kentucky

Wanted to tell you I have been receiving the Ideals *magazine for about 25 years or longer. Thank you so much for a wholesome magazine. I especially enjoy the beautiful pictures.*

Dixie Hogue
Indianapolis, Indiana

* * *   *** * ***

Readers are invited to submit unpublished, original poetry, short anecdotes, and humorous reflections on life for possible publication in future *Ideals* issues. Please send copies only; manuscripts will not be returned. Writers will receive $10 for each published submission. Send materials to "Readers' Reflections," Ideals Publishing Corporation, P.O. Box 140300, Nashville, Tennessee 37214.

Statement of ownership, management, and circulation (Required by 39 U.S.C. 3685), of IDEALS, published eight times a year in February, March, April, June, August, September, November, and December at Nashville, Tennessee, for September, 1988. Publisher, Patricia A. Pingry; Editor, Peggy Schaefer; Managing Editor, as above; Owner, Egmont U.S., Inc., wholly owned subsidiary of The Egmont H. Petersen Foundation, VOGNMAGERGADE 11, 1148 Copenhagen, K, Denmark. The known bondholders, mortgages, and other security holders owning or holding 1 percent or more of total amount of bonds, mortgages, or other securities are: None. Average no. copies each issue during preceding 12 months: Total no. copies printed (Net Press Run) 258,789. Paid circulation 54,842. Mail subscription 190,395. Total paid circulation 245,237. Free distribution 637. Total distribution 245,874. Actual no. copies of single issue published nearest to filing date: Total no. copies printed (Net Press Run) 200,893. Paid circulation 9,871. Mail subscription 176,088. Total paid circulation 185,959. Free distribution 421. Total distribution 186,380. I certify that the statements made by me above are correct and complete. Patricia A. Pingry, Publisher.

ideals

Celebrating Life's Most Treasured Moments